SPINALONGA

The Lepers' Home

Beryl Darby

Typeset and printed in the UK by
Silver Pines Services, Sevenoaks, Kent

First published in 2013 by

JACH Publishing
92 Upper North Street, Brighton, East Sussex, England BN1 3FJ

website: www.beryldarby.co.uk

ACKNOWLEDGEMENTS

I wrote the first guide book to Spinalonga and it was published in 1984. The guide needed to be updated as so much renovation has taken place over there and buildings that were in danger of collapse have been dismantled. There are plans to rebuild some of the old houses using the original materials.

I have to thank Anita Darby and Anna Haynes for their help.

> Anita Darby – for originally contacting a sufferer who had lived on the island and to him for allowing me to use his knowledge.

> Anna Haynes – for providing me with information about the Greek Orthodox Religion and the Churches on the island.

> Sheila Sharman – photographer
> (photographs copyright of Sheila Sharman)

ADDITIONAL SOURCES OF INFORMATION

The Story of Elounda   by George Pediatis

Elounda, Aghios Nikolaos – Spinalonga. Their History
                                    by Manolis Makrakis

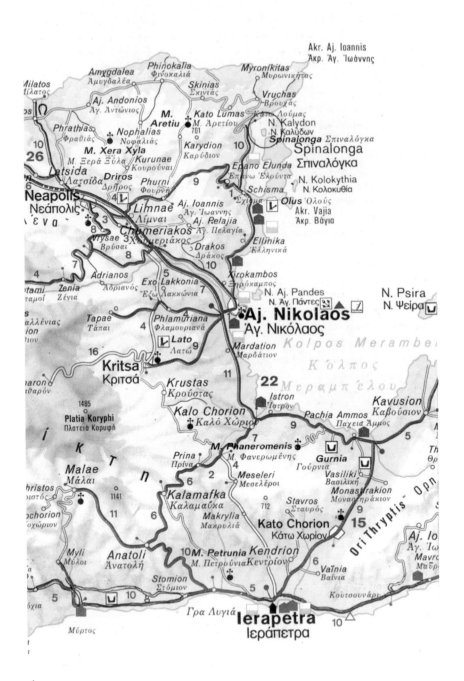

6

INTRODUCTION

The area around the Bay of Mirabello in north eastern Crete has long been renowned for its scenery and has been a popular holiday destination for both Greeks and foreign tourists over many years. Originally Elounda was no more than a small collection of houses slumbering in the sun. The inhabitants gathered salt from the local pans, fished and mined emery to be used as whetstones. Sheep and goats were kept and a small amount of farming was carried out. Their main crop was carob. In 1938 a carob processing factory was built just east of Elounda, the resulting beans, flour and seeds being exported mainly to France and Germany. When Spinalonga was declared a leper colony in 1903 the local villagers supplemented their meagre income by regularly sending over produce and fresh water in their small fishing boats.

The scene is very different today. The village of Plaka, once no more than a collection of derelict houses, has been rebuilt and is now a thriving community of tourist shops and tavernas, with private dwellings mingling with them. Elounda has grown beyond recognition. The area around the small harbour is crammed with shops selling goods of all description from tourist souvenirs to everyday living commodities. There are hotels and self catering apartments on the shore line and stretching back into the hills, jockeying for position with private villas. The town throbs with vibrant life all day and well into the evening and early hours during the summer months.

To experience and recapture the ambience of a true Greek village it is necessary to walk up the hill a short distance and visit Pano Elounda, Kato Elounda or Mavrikiano. These villages are mostly unspoilt by modern development.

During the summer months tourists now flock to Elounda and Plaka, mainly to take a boat over to the island of Spinalonga, to visit the deserted leper colony. My first guide book about the island published in 1984, –

encouraged Melina Mercouri to place a preservation order on the island and there is a street named in her honour in Elounda. There have been various books written about the island which have caught the readers' imagination and they approach their visit to the island with a variety of feelings.

SPINALONGA – HISTORY

Crete has a unique position in the Mediterranean Sea being roughly equidistant from Africa, Asia and Europe. This position placed Crete in the centre of the trade routes and able to benefit from new ideas as they travelled from one continent to another. The island rapidly developed into a centre of art and culture that spread to the mainland of Greece and the other islands.

Due to the affluence and strategic position of the island it became a sought after prize by the all the great powers of the various ages. There are conflicting theories relating to this period of history. Was Crete a province of Egypt or Mycenae or did Crete exact tribute from these centres having originally conquered them? There are reports of the 'Sea People' invading Egypt and these could well have been the Cretans on marauding expeditions.

Around 12000 B.C. the Dorians, a collective name given to the tribes that bordered the northern Greek states, began a southerly migration and invaded Greece. Their knowledge of iron made their weapons superior to those of the occupants of the Greek states, enabling them to conquer and rule the southern area of Greece and spread to the islands.

During the period 12000 – 750 B.C. Crete was in a decline. There are records of climatic changes taking place throughout the world at this time. Were the Minoan palaces and culture destroyed by the Dorians or as a result of the volcanic eruption on Santorini that caused a tsunami to hit Crete? The volcanic ash from the eruption on Santorini would have covered the fertile lands on Crete for many years and pumice would have blocked their harbours. Crete is recorded as having suffered from a famine at this time which in turn led to depopulation and settlements being abandoned.

Whatever the cause of the fall of the Minoan civilization the Dorian people integrated with the island's original inhabitants and a new culture

Spinalonga

finally arose. Art was influenced by contact with the Middle East and led to the period known as the Classical era.

In 66 B.C. the Romans conquered Crete after three years of intensive fighting and added the island to their empire, ruled by Rome until 395 A.D. In 395 A.D. the territories ruled by Rome were divided into East and West and Crete became part of the Byzantine Empire.

Arab Saracens invaded from Spain in 824 A.D. and after taking possession of the island they used it as safe haven when returning from their piratical excursions. One hundred and thirty five years later the Turks laid siege to Chandrax (the old name for Heraklion) for eight months before managing to overthrow the Saracens. Once again Crete became part of the Byzantine Empire and was ruled from Constantinople.

When the Crusaders conquered Constantinople in 1204 A.D. they divided the provinces of the Byzantine Empire between themselves and Crete was sold to the Venetians by the Marquis of Momferato. The Genoese, long time rivals of the Venetians for supremacy at sea, occupied key positions on the island and claimed possession.

For six years the Venetians fought to regain ownership, finally succeeding in 1210 A.D. They immediately began to build fortifications to defend the island from attack. The military experts of the day considered the fortresses they constructed were impregnable.

Despite their strategic positions and strength of construction when the Turks attacked Chania and Rethymnon in 1645 A.D. both fortresses surrendered. The fortress at Heraklion was besieged for twenty one years, the town finally surrendering in 1669 A.D. The only fortress not in the hands of the Turks was the one on Spinalonga.

It was not until 1715 A.D. that the Turks were successful in dislodging the defenders of Spinalonga. The Turks left a skeleton force on the island and they were subsequently joined by their families. The Venetian houses were reconstructed to meet their needs and by 1830 A.D. there were eighty Mohammedan families resident on the island.

Over the next fifty years the population on Spinalonga increased and in the 1881 A.D. census one thousand one hundred and twelve inhabitants are recorded as living there, all of Turkish descent. They claimed their main sources of income as fishing, agriculture and commerce, conveniently omitting to mention smuggling.

When Crete was declared autonomous under the sovereignty of the Sultan the majority of the Turks left the island due to fear of reprisals by the Cretans. In the 1900 A.D. census it is recorded that only three hundred inhabitants remained. Those who remained on Spinalonga felt safe on the island, refusing to leave their homes and they continued with their lucrative smuggling.

Desperate to rid Crete of these outlaws, Prince George passed a resolution in 1903 A.D. declaring Spinalonga was to become a leper colony. Fearful that leprosy sufferers would be sent to live amongst them the Turks left immediately and the first of the sufferers were sent out to the island that the Turks had abandoned.

THE VENETIAN FORTRESS

After the fourth Venetian - Ottoman war ended in 1573 Crete was the Venetians' last colony in the Mediterranean. Desperate to defend their territory and without sufficient finance to repair the seventeen small fortresses that already existed, the Venetians decided to concentrate on fortifying the main ports.

Spinalonga (originally called Kalidon) was selected as a site for a fortress as it sat strategically at the mouth of the sheltered Bay of Elounda where the important salt pans at neighbouring Olous were situated. The island became known as Spinalonga due to the Venetians changing the Greek *eis stin Elounda* (to Elounda) into *spina lunga* (long thorn) due to the shape of the headland

In 1578 Jacobo Foscarini gave the task of designing and erecting a fortress on Spinalonga to the engineer Genese Bressani. The foundation stone (a stone lintel above the gateway to the old port) was laid by General Luca Michiel on 15th June 1579 and it is just possible to decipher the wording.

LUCAS MIC(HAEL) PRO(VISOR) GE(NERALIS)
CR(ETAE) II AN(NO)

Lintel Inscription

Venetian Bastion from the sea

Below the inscription was the sculptured white lion of St. Mark, a symbol of the Venetians' power and possessions, now so weathered it is almost impossible to discern.

The island of Spinalonga was originally a rocky promontory jutting out from the arm of land that runs parallel to the shore from Elounda. The ingenious builders of the fortress incorporated the natural aspects of the rock into their defences. The high defensive walls on the northern and eastern sides of the island are literally built into the rock face, with vertical drops down to the sea. As you sail around the island the cliffs and walls loom above you and again, the white Lion of St Mark is prominently displayed, although now sadly weathered.

Ruins of a fortress, originally built by the Oloundians, to defend their port, were already on the island but these were dismantled and used as land fill for the new fortress. A coastal wall was built around the island, strengthened with bastions and blockhouses. Many improvements to the design were added over the following years until the structure was considered invincible.

Latino Orsini erected more defences on the summit of the island and the fortress was declared completed in 1586. An enormous amount

The Tunnel Entrance

of money had been spent on the construction and numerous deaths were recorded amongst the builders, mostly due to being blown off the scaffolding during high winds.

The design of the fortress is in the shape of an oval, following the contours of Spinalonga. There are only two points of entry. The first is the old port, already mentioned, and the second is a tunnel, sixty four feet long, that leads through the walls to the interior. Both entrances were originally blocked with stout wooden doors, to hinder entry by undesirables.

The long tunnel curves and narrows as it reaches the interior of the fortress. This would have bunched together any invaders, making it difficult for them to use their arms effectively against the defenders.

Once inside the walls there is a flight of steps on the right that leads to a rough path. Behind a narrow arch the path continues until you finally reach the central and highest area of the fortress. The curtain walls, built behind the coastal wall, have the cannon emplacements clearly visible. Half a dozen steps led up to wide cat walks that had been constructed above the emplacements and gave uninterrupted views across the sea for advance warning of invaders. The cat walks would also have been used to give covering fire to the gunners in the event of a landing being successful and an attack taking place.

Having completed the construction of the fortress in 1586 the Venetians blew up the strip of land that joined Spinalonga to the spit of land, effectively making it an island, five hundred metres long and two hundred metres wide at its widest point.

Around three hundred soldiers were garrisoned in the fortress with weaponry consisting of thirty five cannons of various calibre, firearms and light weapons. Provisions were brought out to them from the mainland and they constructed massive water tunnels and cisterns to catch and save rainwater to be used in time of need.

For one hundred and fifty years the fortress guarded the harbour and surrounding area until the Ottomans finally captured it after a siege that

Venetian Water Tunnels

lasted three months. A Treaty was agreed that enabled any guards and inhabitants on the island to leave taking their possessions with them. Unfortunately the Treaty was not honoured. Many Cretans were hung immediately and over six hundred were captured, ending up as galley slaves or sold in the slave market at Heraklion.

Over the years the once impregnable and grand fortress began to crumble. The wind and rain attacked the stone defences; weeds invaded spaces, weakening the interior walls until they collapsed. Stone was salvaged from the piles of rubble for the Turks to repair or build their houses until very little was left of the interior.

Despite so little of the interior of the fortress remaining, a stiff climb up to the summit of the island is rewarding. The buildings of Spinalonga are spread out below you and there is a panoramic view across to the mainland where Plaka and Elounda look like toy villages instead of thriving communities.

LEPROSY

The name 'leprosy' comes from the Greek word 'lepra' meaning scale or scaliness which relates to the skin condition often seen in leprosy sufferers. In Biblical times the diagnosis of leprosy was given to anyone who was suffering from an evident skin condition, and the ailment was believed to have been inflicted on the sufferer as punishment for a sin, making them an outcast from society.

Armauer Hansen, the Norwegian physician, discovered the leprosy bacillus in 1873. He was able to identify the germ in the body, but he did not know how the patient had caught it or how to cure it. Leprosy is now known as Hansen's Disease, having been named after the renowned physician.

Leprosy as we know it today consists of two forms of leprosy bacteria, the Tuberculoid and the Lepromatous. The Tuberculoid form is milder, can be self healing and will respond within a year to the appropriate treatment. The Lepromatous bacillus, although resembling the bacillus associated with Tuberculosis, has a very different effect on the body.

The visible signs of Lepromatous can take anything from ten to thirty years to develop before the patient has visible open wounds. It is a disease of the nerves that attacks the cooler parts of the body; hence the hands and feet are an obvious target.

To the trained medical eye there are four signs that indicate the sufferer has leprosy rather than any other skin condition e.g. psoriasis, eczema, ring worm etc. There will be localised skin patches that have lost much of their pigmentation and appear white. This is particularly noticeable in darker skinned people.   In these areas there will be a sensory deficiency and thickened nerves. (A doctor used to carry a pin in the lapel of his jacket to prick the patient's skin to test for loss of feeling in the area). When a sample is taken from the skin lesions or nasal mucosa, despite containing active Lepromatous bacilli, it is still not possible to cultivate the bacilli under laboratory conditions.

Current treatment for Lepromatous means the disease can be halted within approximately two years. This does not repair the damage that has already occurred in the nerve endings and if physiotherapy does not halt deformity, amputation and plastic surgery often have to be performed to enable the patient to live reasonably independently.

For many years it was thought that the only way to catch leprosy was for an open wound on a healthy person to be in contact with the open sore of sufferer. Recent research has shown that this is not the case. The bacilli live in the respiratory system and cause a runny nose, spreading the bacilli by air born droplets into the area around. Poor living conditions and over-crowding contribute to the spread of the disease, but dietary deficiencies do not appear to be a contributing factor. Research has shown that the armadillo is a carrier of the Lepromatous bacilli.

As the disease progresses massive nodules develop due to the thickening and swelling of the nerves. The swelling leads to cracks and bruising and eventually the open wounds associated with the disease. The nerves eventually shrink and are destroyed in the affected area, causing

Epaminondas Remoundakis

the 'clawed' appearance of the hands. Due to loss of feeling, external injury to the extremities often goes unnoticed leading to severe infections more life threatening than the disease itself.

Prior to 1941 the only known treatment for the disease was Chaulmoogra Oil. Due to research being undertaken at that time a sulphate derivative was developed. Dapsone, taken orally over some years would appear to halt the progress of the disease, but eventually the body would build up a resistance to the medicine. Rifampicin, Clofazimine and Thiacetazone are the most recently developed drugs that appear to be effective in killing the bacilli and halting their destructive progress.

In 1999 the World Health Organization began an experimental programme of B.C.G vaccination in Uganda hoping that as the two diseases – Tuberculosis and Leprosy were akin – this would help to prevent new cases of leprosy and bring the disease under control. At the time 600,000 new cases a year were being diagnosed, which, when the figures were analysed meant 65 new cases per hour, 4 of those would already have a serious disability and 11 would be children. The United States would confirm 100 new cases each year, mainly from Hawaii and Latin America. Males and children appear more susceptible than females and older people. Only five percent of humans in prolonged contact with the bacilli become infected and it is thought this is due a natural immunity.

Despite these horrifying figures from 1999 the number of infected people had dropped considerably by 2011. Due to doctors opening up previously inaccessible regions and treating the sufferers the disease is in check in many areas of the world, although until an effective vaccine is discovered the disease will not be eradicated. It is some consolation to know that only 5% of the world's population are susceptible to the disease, the other 95% have a natural immunity.

During the years 1000 A.D. to 1400 A.D. Great Britain had its highest concentration of leprosy sufferers, probably brought back by the Crusaders. In 1798 the last known case of British leprosy died in the Shetland Islands, although there are some hundreds of known leprosy sufferers living in Britain, all of whom came into the country already suffering from the disease and are receiving treatment. Leprosy is no longer indigent to Britain, but it is a notifiable disease if detected anywhere amongst the community.

LIVING WITH LEPROSY

In 1903 when Prince George declared that the island of Spinalonga was to become a leper colony there was a mass exodus of the Turkish inhabitants. The leprosy sufferers who had been living in caves and shacks in various parts of Crete were gradually found and taken out to the island by the authorities, the first occupants arriving in October 1904. During their journey they would have been jeered and stoned as they passed through the small villages by the healthy inhabitants.

A boatman would have rowed them across the short expanse of water to Spinalonga, whilst they clutched at whatever meagre possessions they had and took a last look at the mainland. Some of the more fortunate would have had a woollen cloak with a hood, a pair of long boots and a change of clothing.

On arriving at the jetty and having been ordered ashore they would lift their downcast eyes to the archway with the inscription carved in to the lintel. The words would mean nothing to them. Slowly they would walk through the arch and up the steps to a path, which was the main road and lined with houses. Here the newcomer would have been able to take their pick of the deserted Venetian and Turkish buildings that were uninhabited. If they were fortunate they could still find an old mattress, table or chair, but little else. They were no worse off than when they had lived in a cave as an outcast and shunned by society.

They were still outcasts. This time they were on a small island, totally dependent upon the villagers from the mainland for their food and water. There was a small natural supply of water from a fountain just inside the main gate, which was just enough to satisfy thirst. Fresh water and food was transported by small boats from the villages of Plaka and Elounda; the arrival of supplies being dependent upon the weather during the winter months and how busy the villagers were with their own affairs.

The old Turkish hospital was used to house the most severely disabled

The Water Fountain

and they were cared for on a daily basis by their fellow sufferers, who would have tended to their every need until their last moment. For four years no doctor visited the island and they had to treat themselves as best they could.

According to the records kept by Dr. Katapoti by 1926 seven hundred and thirty nine patients had been sent to Spinalonga and of these four hundred and sixty five had died. There was only a very small area where it was suitable to bury the dead and this would not have accommodated over four hundred bodies. When a new grave was needed the current occupant was exhumed, the bones washed and the remains thrown down into a tower which became known as the charnel house. Disheartened, disfigured, and often in tremendous pain, one hundred and forty eight men and one hundred and three women lived from day to day doing nothing to better their existence.

Not everyone suffering from leprosy had hidden away, relying on their relatives to provide the necessities to keep them alive. In 1901 a law had been passed creating three leprosy colonies on Crete. Many sufferers submitted voluntarily, expecting to receive medical treatment and care. Over a thousand men and women lived in these centres.

A French Ambassador who was visiting Athens put forward a proposal that all leprosy sufferers should be isolated and contained in one area. He believed this to be the only way to eradicate the disease. Leprosy sufferers from all parts of the Greek mainland were transported to the Pasteur Institute in Athens.

The wards became overcrowded, those originally designed to hold twenty patients now held more than sixty. The water supply and sanitary arrangements were inadequate; the food often rancid or mouldy and insufficient for their needs. When the water supply failed completely water was brought in from other parts of Athens in filthy barrels, often promised and not arriving. The patients felt they had no choice but to accept the neglect and ill treatment.

Finally, with some younger and fitter patients being admitted to the hospital, the inmates decided to protest. Not receiving a satisfactory outcome or any betterment of their conditions they rebelled again, fighting with the orderlies, causing bodily injury to many of them, and also to themselves. When a second rebellion commenced the government sent in soldiers and the ring leaders of the protest were placed in strait jackets and transported to Spinalonga still wearing them.

By then the population on the island had increased to over seven hundred people and accommodation for the newcomers was not available. Due to neglect and an inability of the inhabitants to effect repairs, the houses were becoming ruinous, the walls gradually crumbling and the roofs, mostly made from a mixture of mud and hay, were disintegrating due to the weather.

The most recent arrivals were better educated than many of the original inhabitants and they banded together to form work parties and set about

Laundry and washing troughs

a scheme of renovation and rebuilding, collecting materials from the most dilapidated buildings and re-using them. There was no medical care available to them and they were still reliant upon the mainland villages for their bare necessities.

In an effort to solve the problem of enough fresh water they copied the Venetian idea. Water sheds were constructed from the roofs of their houses enabling the rainwater to be collected in pots and buckets and stored in tanks situated at the far end of the island and a rationing system was put in place. The water was heated on the open fireplaces in the old Turkish laundry area and enabled them to keep their clothes clean.

The women always wanted more water and would creep up the hill at night and steal it. When the men discovered this they guarded the cisterns on a rota basis and the women no longer made their nightly excursions. The guard duty was onerous and the men invented a story about a ghost inhabiting the island at night. Greek people are very superstitious and the women believed the story. As word was spread the Greek ghost became a Negro.

After a few weeks, when no one reported actually seeing the ghost the women became braver again and recommenced their nocturnal visits to the cisterns. As a woman approached one night a black man emerged from behind a rock and waved at her. Naturally the woman screamed and alerted her neighbours. When the inhabitants summoned up enough courage to investigate they found a very frightened, dark skinned Italian who had been left on the island to guard his companions' smuggled goods until their return.

In 1927 Charles Nicolle, the director of the Pasteur Institute in Tunis, visited Spinalonga and he reported on the unsatisfactory conditions he found over there. In his opinion the island was not suitable as a leprosarium. It was suggested that a purpose built hospital be constructed on the long arm of land opposite the mainland.

Despite the interest taken in the conditions of the leprosy sufferers and a desire to better their conditions by the Prime Minister, Eleftherios Venizelos, the building of a new leprosarium was never put into practice. Improvements were made at the hospital and a certain amount of organised reconstruction of the old houses took place at his behest.

A doctor commenced weekly visits, although with the medicines and equipment at his disposal he could do little to ameliorate their suffering. When the doctor had to amputate the arm of a woman suffering from gangrene there was no anaesthetic available and she had to be forcibly held down by her compatriots whilst the doctor sawed off the limb. Likewise, when a young girl appeared to have choked to death one evening she was buried the following day, as was the custom. When her body was exhumed some years later it was found that a terrible mistake had been made. One arm was above her head and her face was turned to the side where she had struggled to make her escape from the grave.

The islanders received a 'pension' of thirty drachmas a month and they were able to use this money to purchase whatever they wished. Soil, seeds, domestic animals, leather, wine and bales of material were just some of the items sent over from the mainland. Gradually small shops were set up along the main street selling surplus produce, others operating as a grocer, butcher, baker, barbers, seamstress, cobblers – the same as in any village on the mainland. There were also four tavernas where an evening

Top: *Interior of Taverna*

Bottom: *The Baker's Premises*

Exterior of Agios Panteleimon

could be passed playing back gammon, cards, chess or just talking over a glass of wine.

There are three churches on Spinalonga, Agios Panteleimon and Agios Yiorgos; the third Agios Nikolaos, is now only recognisable by its foundations. Services were conducted regularly in both buildings, either by the priest who lived on the island (a fellow sufferer) or the one who visited from the mainland.

Marriage between leprosy sufferers was frowned upon thinking it would speed up the progress of the disease, but this was ignored by the islanders. Marriage services were conducted in Agios Panteleimon Church. From these unions thirty nine children were born, but only twenty three survived. It is not known if this was due to the parents being leprous or whether the mortality rate would have been much the same in a mainland village where there was a minimum of medical care. (During this same era in Great Britain child mortality rates are recorded at 13 per 1000).

The parents were allowed to keep their child for two years on the island. After the age of two the child was removed by the authorities and sent to an orphanage in Athens to grow up in healthy surroundings. There are probably a number of elderly people who do not know that their parents were leprosy sufferers and that they were born on Spinalonga.

In 1932 Dr Grammatikakis, as the Governor of Lassithi Province became responsible for the island. He wished to improve the conditions for the people living there and was responsible for the building of the large concrete basins opposite Agios Panteleimon church. Originally these were enclosed against the elements and had open fires to heat the cold water that pipes brought from the cisterns.

The people were also provided with a number of wooden bath tubs that could be filled with the hot water. The inhabitants found an alternative use for these by using them as improvised boats to float across to the mainland. A number of people managed to leave the island by this means. When the authorities discovered the abandoned tubs a full scale search was launched for the escapee and once found they were sent back to Spinalonga. One person was never found by the authorities. As a punishment the bath tubs were confiscated and the villagers were forced to return to washing rather than bathing.

It was at Doctor Grammatikakis's instigation that an electric generator was sent out to the island and placed on the beach outside the fortress walls. This improved conditions immeasurably. No longer were the people dependent upon their dangerous oil lamps for light. Amazingly, when a number of people would have had deformed hands and been unsteady on their feet, there is no record of a fire on the island. Every house on the island was connected to the generator – the white china fitments and wires can still be seen attached to one building – and Spinalonga had electricity long before many villages on the mainland.

In 1936, Epaminondas Remoundakis a third year law student was diagnosed with leprosy and sent to Spinalonga. Despite the conditions on the island having improved over the last thirty two years he was

Original Electrical Fittings

not satisfied. He formed the 'Fraternity of Spinalonga Patients – Agios Panteleimonas' and began to besiege the government with demands. The boatmen no longer needed to be bribed to take a letter to the mainland and post it. Eventually families were given permission to visit their loved ones who had been incarcerated for so long, provided they were disinfected before leaving.

Under his leadership, and with the support of the other well educated inhabitants, the island community was transformed from a place of suffering and neglect. One of the tavernas was turned into a dance hall and concerts, puppet shows and theatre was performed there. A projector was rented and there were regular film shows. The villagers were invited to attend, and after their first apprehension was dispelled, they became frequent visitors, revelling in the activities taking place.

A library was created and a newspaper produced, called the 'Satire' which was eagerly awaited each week by the inhabitants. It not only contained news of forthcoming attractions at the dance hall, but also humorous articles about events that had occurred on the island. From being a sad, apathetic collection of sick people, the island now housed over two thousand people who went about their business each day as they would have done in any village on the mainland. They had become a community to which they were proud to belong.

In 1937 Dr Grammatikakis arranged for a new hospital and laboratory to be built up on the hill of the island, planning to have it staffed by doctors and technicians who commuted daily from the mainland. Despite having

The Hospital

The new Flats built in 1948

the building facilities in place, Chaulmoogra Oil and Dapsone were still the only medicines available, and often neither supplies nor doctors could reach the island due to bad weather.

When the Germans invaded Crete in May 1941 they spread out across Crete. Upon reaching Elounda and Plaka they left a battalion of Italian soldiers to guard the area with instructions that no one was to go out to Spinalonga. The Germans anticipated the island would be an ideal rendezvous for resistance groups.

Cut off from supplies from the mainland, the villagers were forced to survive on whatever produce they were able to grow. Gradually their few sheep, goats and chickens were slaughtered and the vegetables eaten. There was no bread, no oil and no wine. They gathered shell fish from the rocks to flavour water for their subsistence meals, their bodies growing weaker daily. When the island was finally relieved in October 1944 there were only forty inhabitants left alive. Epaminondas Remoundakis was one of them.

Teams of workmen were sent over to Spinalonga, but many of the buildings were in such a bad state of repair and neglect that they were abandoned to the elements. As more sufferers were diagnosed and sent to Spinalonga once again there became a housing shortage and in 1948 the Government built two blocks of flats. Each block contained twenty

Communal Kitchens in the new Flats

four rooms and four kitchens, plastered walls, running water and electric light, but they were not popular with the older residents who preferred their original homes and refused to move.

In 1954 change was afoot again as the Government decided it was no longer viable to keep Spinalonga open as a leprosarium and negotiations began to move the two hundred and twenty seven sufferers to the hospital of Aghia Varvara in Athens. Finally in 1957 the proposed move took place for the thirty lepers who still lived on Spinalonga. It was with great reluctance and sadness that they left their island home.

Medicine had improved over the intervening years and tests showed that in many cases the disease had halted – burnt out – and the person was no threat to the community. This enabled some of the patients to return to their original homes, but most opted to stay in the security of the hospital, free to travel amongst the Athenians as they pleased.

It is customary in the Greek Orthodox religion to say commemorative prayers for the dead at regular intervals – after forty days, six months, one year, three years and finally five years. One person had died a month before the island was evacuated and to complete his religious obligations to the dead, Father Chrisanthos remained alone on Spinalonga until 1962.

Agios Yiorgo Church

EXPLORING THE ISLAND

As the boat crosses the bay from Elounda, the island looms ever larger and you are able to imagine the feelings of the sufferers who were taken there to live out the remainder of their lives. For many years they were denied contact with their relatives and friends and were totally dependent upon their food and water from the mainland.

It is no longer possible to go ashore from your boat at the old jetty as it has become silted up and unsuitable for the larger boats that now make the regular trip. Instead you land at a small, open area of beach outside the fortress walls. Originally the generator stood here and its place has now been taken by a small taverna with drinks and ice cream available. There are also toilet facilities and an emergency telephone to alert the mainland if anyone should inadvertently remain on the island after the last boat of the day has departed. A small kiosk sells entrance tickets and the revenue from this provides some of the finance needed to restore and repair the island.

The ideal way to explore the island is 'from the beginning to the end'. First mount the shallow steps leading to the tunnel that is the old entrance to the fortress. The iron gate is a modern addition which is closed at the end of the day and when the island is not open to the public. The walls of the fortress walls tower above you and you leave the harsh sunlight and walk sixty five feet through a cool, dim passage until you enter the village square.

Behind you, on the right, is an old water fountain. This was the only source of fresh water available to the leprosy sufferers when they lived on the island. Water no longer runs from it and two brass fittings cap off the outlets. If you walk to the right and mount the steps the foundations of the old houses that were built over the tunnel are clearly visible. The inhabitants who once lived up there would have had a magnificent view across the sea to both Elounda and Plaka.

The Village Square

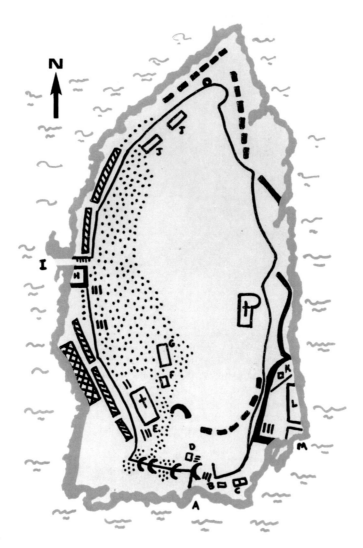

Key

▬	Venetian Construction	F	Dispensary
▬	Modern Construction	G	Hospital
▨	Venetian Water Tunnels	H	Disinfection Room
▧	Laundry	I	Original Port and Entrance
A	Concrete Jetty	J	Flats
B	Concrete Generator Base	K	Charnal House
C	Cinema	L	Graveyard
D	Re-constructed House	M	Carpenter's House
E	Quarry Area	⋰⋱	Area Occupied by Lepers

The Village Square (with the doors restored)

Top: *Steps leading to the area above the tunnel*

Bottom: *A Restored House*

The main street leading from the Square

The main street

Looking across the main street from inside a house

View across the Square from inside a house

Retrace your steps back down to the square and look to the right. Half way up a flight of steps that lead to the upper part of the fortress, a two storey house has been repaired and given new shutters, balcony and door. This is how the houses would have looked when they were first constructed by the Venetians or Ottomans.

The buildings around the square have been cleared of weeds and rubbish and made safe for visitors to enter and explore. The remaining walls show the size of the rooms and the paved or earthen floor. Sadly, where so much has had to be demolished, the two storey house that had lost some of its external rendering is no longer there. The walls clearly showed how battens had been fixed between stronger supports and loose stones piled up to form a wall that was subsequently covered with cement. Fortunately there is still another further down the road.

The house next door has an arched doorway and windows that were originally painted red. The cupboard and stairs that could once be seen inside have again been removed and only the bare walls remain. Opposite is a tall building with long double doors, originally hinged to fold back externally, the hook to hold them still in place. A yucca tree at the side has grown to magnificent proportions, stretching up to the archway that was once an integral part of the fortress.

Building methods used in original construction

Άποψη του κεντρικού δρόμου κατά τη δεκαετία του '70
View of the main street in the 1970s

The main street before restoration

As you pass under this arch you are in the main street. This is where the parade of shops was situated. From these small buildings the lepers displayed whatever produce they had to offer for sale to the community. One pair of old wooden shutters (now replaced) had the date 1940 scratched inside and the letters TETRE-AOE- outside along with carvings of small ships. This area has now been restored and is the Education Centre for the island.

Restored main street, now the Education Centre

There are displays of artefacts and information in each room, but very little information or space is devoted to the time the lepers occupied Spinalonga. The new shutters have been brightly painted in different colours and the whole area has taken on a very different appearance and feeling from its previous ruinous state.

The final building in the row has fourteen stone steps on the outside. These would have led to a flat roof or possibly another room. The homes or shops that originally sat opposite have been removed and the area that was used by the lepers to quarry larger blocks of stone has gone. In spring and summer the quarry had been a riot of colour with roses, geraniums and daisies flourishing.

Standing next to the quarry is the Church of Agios Panteleimon. This Saint's Name Day falls on 27th July and is celebrated each year by the inhabitants of Elounda and Plaka who come over to Spinalonga. This church was used on a regular basis for weekly services, marriages and christenings when the lepers lived on the island.

At one time it was only possible to peer through dirty windows at the interior, but that has changed. It has been cleaned and painted, the altar

The interior of Agios Panteleimon Church

area refurbished and you can buy a candle to light in memory of a loved one. The church bell has been placed on a mount a short distance away and is no longer rung by pulling on an old, frayed rope.

Take a detour up the steps beside the church and you will come to the old hospital building. Here old and tattered curtains still flutter at some of the windows. Look inside and you can see a stone sink and stone bench. Was this the operating theatre where so many people underwent amputation under primitive conditions?

Across the road from the church the first of the Venetian water tunnels can be reached by mounting seven steps. There are two inspection chambers that are now safely covered, whereas at one time, you could look down and see water far below. Between the old wall of the fortress and the water tunnel is the laundry. When Dr. Grammatakis had this constructed it consisted of two rooms, one containing fourteen basins and six fireplaces for heating water and the other having ten basins and four fireplaces. When first constructed the building was protected from the elements with a roof; but that has long since disintegrated.

Walking past the church there are the remains of some of the old Venetian houses. Their secluded gardens can be accessed through arches

Toilet Building

Interior of toilet

and gateways. It is obvious by the plants and shrubs that are still growing here that the gardens were once cared for and well tended. Unfortunately, due to self seeding, many of the small trees had found a home between cracks in walls and paving and have had to be removed. Beside the garden entrances are small, semi-circular outbuildings, their curved walls projecting out onto the road. These are ground level toilets, constructed on the old Turkish soak-away system and in some the remains of wooden seats can be seen.

At the end of the row of houses, on the left side, there is a large building that was a part of the fortress when it was manned. There is an opening where you can look through at the dark and dismal place down below. Walk down the steps leading to the old port and you are able to enter this solid structure that was converted by the Health Authorities into a disinfection room. All items and visitors that left the island to make the journey to the mainland had to be disinfected in here before permission was granted for them or the goods to leave.

The Disinfection Room

Continue down to the old jetty where the lepers would have disembarked and where their food and water was delivered. Again a gate has been placed across the entrance that can be closed to restrict the access of the public. No longer can you swim or sail over and experience walking around alone to absorb the atmosphere at night.

Walk slowly along the road, taking detours between the buildings on the paths that have now been cleared and made further buildings available to the public. You can still see the remains of painted plaster on some of the walls; one has a blue frieze in evidence. There are rotting staircases, cupboards with their doors sagging dangerously, shutters that hang precariously and the sunlight streams through the holes in the roofs. In many cases the timbers that once supported the upper floor are now lying in a tangled heap on the ground.

A side road

Fireplace below with oven above

In some houses remnants of rags had been stuffed between the stones of the walls to stop draughts and others had pinned cardboard beneath their windows as a draught excluder. The tavernas where the lepers were able to relax and spend their evenings are distinguishable by the wide arches leading to their back rooms and the large open fireplaces are clearly visible.

The ovens, set half way up the walls for ease of access, were used by the bakers and also as communal ovens where people could take their meal to be cooked. This practice is continued in some of the villages today.

Finally you reach the end of the village street where the two separate blocks of modern flats were constructed. They consisted of small individual rooms and communal kitchens; the only difference between them was their exterior colour; one was painted pale blue and the other cream. The colours have now faded and both are a dirty grey. They are part of the programme of renovation and reconstruction that is taking place continually and it would be interesting if one room was decorated and furnished in the period showing their amenities.

A short distance up the road from the flats is an ammunition tower on the seaward side. Here the road becomes rougher and curves around the end of the island. Despite the overgrown fortress ramparts a cat walk can

Venetian Bastion from the sea

be seen, its protective walls having a sheer drop into the sea below. There are no houses on this side of the island as there is no shelter from the wind blowing across the open sea from Rhodes. Here you walk past one of the original walls constructed by the Venetians when they first fortified the island and can also view the northern part of the fortress where it juts out into the sea. An engineering accomplishment completed by the original builders to be admired.

A little lower down is the Turkish graveyard. There are no gravestones or markers, just a simple sign announcing its purpose. The lepers never tried to utilise this area for their own burials. Not only did they have a respect for the dead who already occupied the ground, they had no wish to be buried amongst the Turks.

From here you can see the small church of Agios Yiorgos nestling into the hillside on the right hand side. Unfortunately the two cypress trees that once grew here have been removed. It was from this church that the lepers conducted their burial service and subsequent interment. A few yards further on from the church, on the seaward side, a flight of steps lead up to the graveyard. Beside the graveyard area there is a small building that the island carpenter used as his workshop. There he made the coffins and the crosses for those who were able to pay for their burial. Up here is the small area that contains the graves laid out in a grid pattern.

All the graves are of a regular size and with an even distance between them. Sadly it became necessary to seal them to prevent souvenir hunters from removing anything from inside. Originally you could walk between them and over to the tower that was the charnel house. Once your eyes had become accustomed to the interior darkness you could distinguish the remains the remains of the lepers who could not afford an individual grave, and those who were exhumed after four years. This whole area has been cleared of weeds and roped off to the public whilst repair to the charnel house takes place. Sadly, when I was there last, people appeared more curious about the area where the lepers were buried than where they had lived.

This is a place to stand, contemplate and respect the men and women who lived and died over here. Through their tenacity and bravery they could be proud to declare they had lived on Spinalonga.

The Graveyard

I hope you enjoyed your visit to Spinalonga.

If you wish to know more about the life of the men and women who were sent to the island to spend the rest of their lives as outcasts do read the compelling story of **YANNIS**.

The book tells the heart-rending and authentic account of a man's life on the small island, his struggle for survival, his loves and losses, along with that of his family on the mainland from 1918 to 1979.

"Wonderful characterisation – all the flavour of local Cretan life – brilliant telling of a story based on actual events – probably the most moving novel I have ever read."
Roger Wickham

"I sat up most of one night reading. I literally could not put this book down."
Eileen Bradley

Other books in the Cretan family saga by Beryl Darby:-
ANNA GIOVANNI JOSEPH CHRISTABELLE SAFFRON NICOLA

Complementing the 'family' series
MANOLIS CATHY VASI ALECOS